Culture); DOING BIRD (Cat 'A' Theatre & UK Tour); PLAYBOY OF THE
WESTERN WORLD (Communicado); THE STINGING SEA (Citizens'
Theatre); TARTUFFE (Dundee Rep); JOLLY ROBERT/GLORIA GOODHEART
(Theatre Workshop); HAMLET (National Theatre Workshop). Television
work includes: TAGGART (STV); REBUS (Clerkenwell Films); PSYCHOS
(Channel 4); LIFE SUPPORT, A MUG'S GAME, STRATHBLAIR, THE
FERGUSON THEORY, RAB C NESBITT, TAKIN' OVER THE ASYLUM,
TREV AND SIMON (BBC); THE BILL (Thames). Film includes:
AFTERLIFE (Gabriel Films); RATCATCHER (Holy Cow Films); STELLA
DOES TRICKS (Channel 4); KARMIC MOTHERS (Fresh Films).

Michael Moreland (*John*) For the Traverse: GAGARIN WAY. Other
theatre includes: STROMA (TAG); PASSING PLACES (Greenwich
Theatre); JUNK (Oxford Stage Company); THE COUNTRY WIFE
(Bridewell Theatre); THE SEAL WIFE (Attic Theatre Company); WOOF
(Birmingham Stage Company); MACBETH (Gateway Theatre, Chester).
Television work includes: THE BILL, MURDER PREVENTION, A TOUCH
OF FROST (ITV); MONARCH OF THE GLEN, CASUALTY, THE BELLROCK
(BBC). Film includes: 16 YEARS OF ALCOHOL (16 Years Ltd); THE
TRENCH (Portman Productions); A TIME TO LOVE (Hungry Eye).

Adam Reeves (*Found Man*) Trained at School of Drama at
Queen Margaret University College, Edinburgh. Theatre credits
include: THE LIFE OF JESUS CHRIST (Dundas Castle Estate) and work
on Rehearsal Room readings with Stellar Quines. QMUC credits
include: TINY DYNAMITE, THE WINTER'S TALE and TRANSLATIONS.

Siobhan Reilly (*Agnes*) Trained at RSAMD. Theatre credits
include: SNUFF (Arches Theatre Company) and LITTLE SNOW WHITE
(Cumbernauld Theatre). RSAMD theatre credits include: THE CHERRY
ORCHARD, PERIDES, TARTUFFE and IVANOV.

John Stahl (*Rafter*) For the Traverse: MR PLACEBO (co-production
with Drum Theatre Plymouth), GAGARIN WAY, THE MEETING (co-
production with EIF), ANNA WEISS, SHINING SOULS, THE
ARCHITECT. Other theatre includes: PROFESSOR BERNHARDI (Oxford
Stage Company/Dumbfounded Theatre); TAMAR'S REVENGE, DOG
IN THE MANGER, PEDRO THE GREAT PRETENDER (RSC); HAMLET
(Belgrave); SARJEANT MUSGRAVE'S DANCE, BREAD AND BUTTER
(Oxford Stage Company); CRAVE (Paines Plough); ALL MY SONS
(Theatre Royal, Plymouth); THE REAL WURLD, THE BABY, PADDY'S
MARKET, MACBETH (The Tron). Television work includes: THE DARIEN
VENTURE, DOCTORS, MURDER ROOMS, GLASGOW KISS (BBC);
DR FINLAY (ITV); TAGGART, HIGH ROAD (STV). Film includes: LOCH
NESS (Polygram/Working Title).

Ros Steen (Voice/Dialect Coach): Trained: RSAMD. Has worked extensively in theatre, film and TV. For the Traverse: IN THE BAG, THE SLAB BOYS TRILOGY, DARK EARTH, HOMERS, OUTLYING ISLANDS, THE BALLAD OF CRAZY PAOLA, THE TRESTLE AT POPE LICK CREEK, HERITAGE (2001 and 1998), AMONG UNBROKEN HEARTS, SHETLAND SAGA, SOLEMN MASS FOR A FULL MOON IN SUMMER (as co-director), KING OF THE FIELDS, HIGHLAND SHORTS, FAMILY, KILL THE OLD TORTURE THEIR YOUNG, THE CHIC NERDS, GRETA, LAZYBED, KNIVES IN HENS, PASSING PLACES, BONDAGERS, ROAD TO NIRVANA, SHARP SHORTS, MARISOL, GRACE IN AMERICA. Other theatre credits includes: TWELFTH NIGHT, DANCING AT LUGHNASA, DUCHESS OF MALFI, (Dundee Rep); BASH, DAMN JACOBITE BITCHES, OBSERVE THE SONS OF ULSTER MARCHING TOWARDS THE SOMME (Citizens' Theatre); WORD FOR WORD (Magnetic North); CAVE DWELLERS (7:84); EXILES (Jerwood Young Directors/Young Vic); THE PRIME OF MISS JEAN BRODIE, PLAYBOY OF THE WESTERN WORLD (Royal Lyceum, Edinburgh). Film credits include: THE ADVENTURES OF GREYFRIARS BOBBY (Piccadilly Pictures); GREGORY'S TWO GIRLS (Channel Four Films). Television credits include: SEA OF SOULS, ROCKFACE, 2000 ACRES OF SKY (BBC).

Philip Wilson (Director & Designer) Recent directorial credits include: UN UOMO TROVATO – a version of THE FOUND MAN in Italian (Teatro della Limonaia, Sesto Fiorentino); AIN'T MISBEHAVIN' (Sheffield Crucible); DR FAUSTUS, THE ASTONISHED HEART & STILL LIFE (Liverpool Playhouse); BREAKING THE CODE (Theatre Royal, Northampton) and AS YOU LIKE IT (British International Theatre Program, Florida). As Artistic Director of Stage d'Or Theatre Company, his credits included directing THE HUMOROUS LIEUTENANT (BAC) and BLOODY POETRY (Troubadour Crypt) and directing and designing THE QUEEN AND THE REBELS (Courtyard Theatre). Other director/designer credits include THE MAKING OF MISS PEGGY LEE (BAC) and MARAT/SADE (Avondale Hall). Philip was Associate Director for ARSENIC AND OLD LACE (Strand Theatre) and HAMLET (West Yorkshire Playhouse) and Assistant Director for ROMEO AND JULIET (RSC Regional and World Tour). He was awarded a Regional Theatre Young Director Scheme bursary in 1995, and spent 18 months at Greenwich Theatre. Film and TV credits include: Performance Consultant on SHAKESPEARE IN LOVE (Miramax/Universal); two years as a producer in the Entertainment department of the BBC. Writing includes: translations of NAKED (Luigi Pirandello) and THE QUEEN AND THE REBELS (Ugo Betti) and an adaptation for the stage of J.L. Carr's A MONTH IN THE COUNTRY.

SCOTLAND'S NEW WRITING THEATRE

Traverse Theatre Company

The Found Man

by Riccardo Galgani

cast in order of appearance

Rafter	John Stahl
Moffat	Liam Brennan
John Gear	Michael Moreland
Mary Gear	Molly Innes
Agnes	Siobhan Reilly
Found Man	Adam Reeves

Director & Designer	Philip Wilson
Assistant Director	Christopher Haydon
Lighting Designer	Neil Austin
Sound Designer	Gareth Fry
Voice/Dialect Coach	Ros Steen
Stage Manager	Lee Davis
Deputy Stage Manager	Gemma Smith
Assistant Stage Manager	Jenny Raith
Wardrobe Supervisor	Aileen Sherry

First performed at the Traverse Theatre, Edinburgh, on Friday 29 July 2005

TRAVERSE THEATRE

Powerhouse of new writing DAILY TELEGRAPH

Artistic Director Philip Howard

The Traverse is Scotland's new writing theatre. Founded in 1963 by a group of maverick artists and enthusiasts, it began as an imaginative attempt to capture the spirit of adventure and experimentation of the Edinburgh Festival all year round. Throughout the decades, the Traverse has evolved and grown in artistic output and ambition. It has refined its mission by strengthening its commitment to producing new plays by Scottish and international playwrights and actively nurturing them throughout their careers. Traverse productions have been seen worldwide and tour regularly throughout the UK and overseas.

The Traverse has produced over 600 new plays in its lifetime and, through a spirit of innovation and risk-taking, has launched the careers of many of the country's best known writers. From, among others, Stanley Eveling in the 1960s, John Byrne in the 1970s, Liz Lochhead in the 1980s, to David Greig and David Harrower in the 1990s, the Traverse is unique in Scotland in its dedication to new writing. It fulfils the crucial role of providing the infrastructure, professional support and expertise to ensure the development of a dynamic theatre culture for Scotland.

The Traverse's activities encompass every aspect of playwriting and production, providing and facilitating play reading panels, script development workshops, rehearsed readings, public playwriting workshops, writers' groups, discussions and special events. The Traverse's work with young people is of supreme importance and takes the form of encouraging playwriting through its flagship education project *Class Act*, as well as the Traverse Young Writers' Group. In 2004, the Traverse took the Class Act project to Russia and also staged *Articulate*, a pilot project with West Dunbartonshire Council for 11 to 14 year olds.

Edinburgh's Traverse Theatre is a mini-festival in itself THE TIMES

From its conception in the 1960s, the Traverse has remained a pivotal venue during the Edinburgh Festival. It receives enormous critical and audience acclaim for its programming, as well as regularly winning awards. In 2001 the Traverse was awarded two Scotsman Fringe Firsts and two Herald Angels for its own productions of *Gagarin Way* and *Wiping My Mother's Arse* and a Herald Archangel for overall artistic excellence. In 2002 the Traverse produced award-winning shows, *Outlying Islands* by David Greig and *Iron* by Rona Munro and in 2003, *The People Next Door* by Henry Adam picked up Fringe First and Herald Angel awards before transferring to the Theatre Royal, Stratford East. Re-cast and with a new director, *The People Next Door* has since toured to Germany, the Balkans and New York. In 2004, the Traverse produced the award-winning *Shimmer* by Linda McLean and a stage adaptation of Raja Shehadeh's diary account of the Israeli occupation of Ramallah, *When The Bulbul Stopped Singing*. This play won the Amnesty International Freedom of Expression Award 2004, appeared in January 2005 as part of the Fadjr International Theatre Festival in Tehran and toured to New York in Spring 2005.

To find out about ways to support the Traverse, please contact Norman MacLeod, Development Manager on 0131 228 3223.
www.traverse.co.uk

COMPANY BIOGRAPHIES

Neil Austin (Lighting Designer) For the Traverse: FURTHER THAN THE FURTHEST THING, THE PEOPLE NEXT DOOR, DARK EARTH, MR PLACEBO (co-production with Drum Theatre Plymouth). Other theatre includes: HENRY IV PTS.1&2, FIX UP, A PRAYER FOR OWEN MEANY, THE NIGHT SEASON, THE WALLS, FURTHER THAN THE FURTHEST THING (National Theatre); JULIUS CAESAR, TWO GENTLEMEN OF VERONA (Royal Shakespeare Company); THE COSMONAUT'S LAST MESSAGE..., HENRY IV, WORLD MUSIC, AFTER MISS JULIE, CALIGULA (Donmar Warehouse); MACBETH (Almeida); FLESH WOUND, TRUST (Royal Court); JAPES (Theatre Royal, Haymarket); A LIFE IN THE THEATRE (Apollo, West End); CUCKOOS (BITE, Barbican); INSIGNIFICANCE, CLOUD NINE, THE MODERNISTS, WORLD MUSIC (Crucible, Sheffield); TWELFTH NIGHT, TRUE WEST, GREAT EXPECTATIONS (Bristol Old Vic); AMERICAN BUFFALO (Royal Exchange, Manchester); THE WIND IN THE WILLOWS, PRETENDING TO BE ME, THE LADY IN THE VAN (West Yorkshire Playhouse); CHIMPS, STILL LIFE, THE ASTONISHED HEART, ROMEO & JULIET, TWELFTH NIGHT (Liverpool Playhouse). Dance includes: RHAPSODY (Royal Ballet, Royal Opera House); DARKNESS & LIGHT (Tokyo & Nagoya Expo); THE SOLDIER'S TALE (ROH2, Linbury Theatre). Opera includes: THE CRICKET RECOVERS, MAN AND BOY: DADA, THE EMBALMER (Almeida Opera); CHORUS! (Welsh National Opera); L'ORFEO (Opera City, Tokyo); PULSE SHADOWS (Queen Elizabeth Hall).

Liam Brennan (Moffat) For the Traverse: SOLEMN MASS FOR A FULL MOON, QUARTZ, THE SPECULATOR, FAMILY, KNIVES IN HENS, WORMWOOD. Other theatre includes: ANNA KARENINA, OTHELLO, THINGS WE DO FOR LOVE, THE GOWK STORM, TAMING OF THE SHREW (Royal Lyceum, Edinburgh); EDWARD II/RICHARD II; MEASURE FOR MEASURE, TWELFTH NIGHT/THE GOLDEN ASS, MACBETH (Shakespeare's Globe); seasons and productions with Sheffield Crucible, Perth Rep, Dundee Rep, Citizens, Borderline, Cumbernauld Theatre, 7:84, Salisbury Playhouse, Calypso Theatre, Dublin, Durham Theatre Co and The Brunton. Television work includes: TAGGART, HIGH ROAD (STV); BAD BOYS, MACHAIR, STRATHBLAIR (BBC). Film includes: NO MAN'S LAND (Hopscotch Films); FEET STEPS (Shortfilm Factory); GAS ATTACK (Insight TV Ltd, winner of the Michael Powell Best Film Award). Liam has recorded numerous plays and short stories for BBC Radio 4.

Riccardo Galgani (Writer) Born in Glasgow in 1969. THE FOUND MAN is Riccardo's third play for the Traverse, following ACTS (part of the FAMILY trilogy, 1999) and GREEN FIELD (2002). Riccardo was awarded the 2002 Pearson Bursary for Playwright in

Residence at the Traverse Theatre. In addition to his work for theatre, Riccardo has written and directed two short films. He has also done adaptation and rewriting work for film as well as developing feature length projects of his own.

Gareth Fry (Sound Designer) Trained at the Central School of Speech & Drama in Theatre Design. For the Traverse: MR PLACEBO (co-production with Drum Theatre Plymouth). Other theatre credits as a sound designer and occasionally as a composer include: NOISE OF TIME (Complicite with the Emerson String Quartet); THEATRE OF BLOOD (Lyttleton Theatre); TALKING TO TERRORISTS (Out of Joint); ASTRONAUT (Theatre O); CHIMPS (Liverpool Playhouse). Other work includes: STRANGE POETRY (with the LA Philharmonic Orchestra); MNEMONIC (associate); GENOA 01 (Complicite); FIX UP, IPHIGENIA AT AULIS, THE THREE SISTERS, IVANOV, THE ORESTEIA (National Theatre, UK); FORTY WINKS, UNDER THE WHALEBACK, NIGHT SONGS, FACE TO THE WALL, REDUNDANT, MOUNTAIN LANGUAGE, ASHES TO ASHES, THE COUNTRY (Royal Court); WORLD MUSIC, THE DARK (Donmar Warehouse); GISELLE (Fabulous Beast); MACBETH (Out of Joint); BY THE BOG OF CATS (Wyndhams Theatre); BLITHE SPIRIT (Savoy Theatre); ZERO DEGREES AND DRIFTING (Unlimited Theatre); TIME AND SPACE (Living Dance Studio, Beijing); SHAPE OF METAL (Abbey, Dublin); LIVING COSTS (DV8 at Tate Modern); THE WATERY PART OF THE WORLD (BAC); MIDSUMMER NIGHTS DREAM (Regents Park Open Air Theatre); ECCENTRICITIES OF A NIGHTINGALE (Gate, Dublin); FORBIDDEN BROADWAY (Albery); HOLY MOTHERS (New Ambassadors); ACCRINGTON PALS (Chichester); WEXFORD TRILOGY (OSC); PLAY TO WIN (Yellow Earth). Gareth also designs the music and sound systems for Somerset House's ice rink.

Christopher Haydon (Assistant Director) Trained: The Central School of Speech and Drama and Cambridge University. Central theatre credits include: (as director) COME AND GO, THE MAIDS, AGAMEMNON; (as actor) TIN DRUM, THE BALCONY, PILLOWTALK.

Molly Innes (*Mary Gear*) For the Traverse: ONE DAY ALL THIS WILL COME TO NOTHING, THE SLAB BOYS TRILOGY, GREEN FIELD, SOLEMN MASS FOR A FULL MOON, WIDOWS, SHINING SOULS, STONES AND ASHES. Other theatre includes: GOOD THINGS (Borderline/Byre/Perth Rep); THE MEMORY OF WATER, WIT (Stellar Quines); THE GOOD WOMAN OF SETZUAN, ANTIGONE (TAG); PLASTICINE (Royal Court); BLOODED (Boilerhouse); A LISTENING HEAVEN, JEKYLL AND HYDE, TO KILL A MOCKING BIRD, THE PRIME OF MISS JEAN BRODIE (Royal Lyceum, Edinburgh); TIMELESS (Suspect

SPONSORSHIP

Sponsorship income enables the Traverse to commission and produce new plays and to offer audiences a diverse and exciting programme of events throughout the year. We would like to thank the following companies for their support:

CORPORATE SPONSORS

B B C Scotland

tv productions

LUMISON

pinnacle
communications ltd

THE HALLION

NICHOLAS
GROVES
RAINES
ARCHITECTS

CHAMPAGNE
ALAIN THIENOT
REIMS · FRANCE

ANNIVERSARY ANGELS

With thanks to

Claire Aitken of Royal Bank of Scotland for mentoring support
arranged through the Arts & Business Mentoring Scheme.
Purchase of the Traverse Box Office, computer network and
technical and training equipment has been made possible with
money from The Scottish Arts Council National Lottery Fund

The Traverse Theatre's work
would not be possible without the support of

The Traverse Theatre receives financial assistance from

The Calouste Gulbenkian Foundation, The Peggy Ramsay Foundation, The Binks Trust, The Bulldog Prinsep Theatrical Fund, The Esmée Fairbairn Foundation, The Gordon Fraser Charitable Trust, The Garfield Weston Foundation, The Paul Hamlyn Foundation, The Craignish Trust, Lindsay's Charitable Trust, The Tay Charitable Trust, The Ernest Cook Trust, The Wellcome Trust, The Sir John Fisher Foundation, The Ruben and Elisabeth Rausing Trust, The Equity Trust Fund, The Cross Trust, N Smith Charitable Settlement, Douglas Heath Eves Charitable Trust, The Bill and Margaret Nicol Charitable Trust, The Emile Littler Foundation, Mrs M Guido's Charitable Trust, Gouvernement du Québec, The Canadian High Commission, The British Council, The Daiwa Foundation, The Sasakawa Foundation, The Japan Foundation

Charity No. SC002368

Sets, props and costumes for
THE FOUND MAN
created by Traverse Workshops
(funded by the National Lottery)

Scottish
Arts Council
LOTTERY FUNDED

Production photography by Douglas Robertson
Print photography by Euan Myles

For their continued generous support
of Traverse productions the Traverse thanks

Habitat, Marks and Spencer, Princes Street
Camerabase, BHS, and Holmes Place

For their help on THE FOUND MAN, the Traverse thanks

The cast, crew and creative team on UN UOMO TROVATO
(the Italian version of THE FOUND MAN) and all the staff at
Teatro della Limonaia, Sesto Fiorentino – with special thanks to
Daniel Dwerryhouse, Gloria Amaranti and Fiamma Arrighi;
RSAMD; Dundee Rep.

Riccardo Galgani would like to thank

Philip Howard, for his invaluable support and belief. Everyone at the
Traverse for their untiring work. Roxana Silbert for her input and
continuing enthusiasm. And special thanks to my wife and my mother.

TRAVERSE THEATRE – THE COMPANY

THE FOUND MAN

Riccardo Galgani

Characters

JAMES MOFFAT, *forty*

AGNES LESLIE MOFFAT, *fifteen*

CHARLES RAFTER, *sixty*

MARY GEAR, *thirty*

JOHN GEAR, *thirty*

A MAN WHO IS FOUND, *twenty-four*

Time, Setting and Staging

The time is circa 1859.

The play takes place on the coast, within an isolated, rural community.

The residents are native to that community.

The stage is an open space, broader at the front than at the back, extending as far to the rear as possible and giving a great sense of depth.

The set requires an absolute simplicity, with nothing other than what is used or referred to on the stage. The things that are used ought to give an impression of an inherent roughness and impoverishment.

The dress is neutral and pragmatic in style.

The play is to be performed without an interval.

1.

In the centre, the frame of a door.

At the front, a carpenter's work stand.

MOFFAT *enters, carrying several lengths of wood.*

He places the wood against the side wall, takes one length, and puts it on the stand. He begins to saw.

RAFTER *enters from the back of the stage, as though from a steep slope (unseen). He is walking with the aid of a stick and holding a piece of paper. He is in high spirits.*

RAFTER. Good day Moffat.

MOFFAT. Rafter.

RAFTER. The walk up here doesn't get any easier.

MOFFAT. Not by much.

RAFTER. Not by any I'd say!

MOFFAT. You didn't have to take it.

RAFTER. The boat's just come in.

MOFFAT (*stopping work*). Is there some news?

    RAFTER *brandishes the piece of paper.*

RAFTER. It's brought notice.

MOFFAT. About Sinclair?

RAFTER. He's written here, his furniture's arrived as well.

MOFFAT. He must be near then.

RAFTER (*with excitement*). The day after tomorrow he says. We can welcome him at the pier then. I'll put some posters in the square. Get the town to bring him up to his house. (*Beat.*) Is it nearly done?

MOFFAT. Almost.

RAFTER. You must be finishing by now?

MOFFAT. I'm making a start on the door.

RAFTER (*his mood turning*). You're starting?

MOFFAT. Don't worry yourself about it Rafter. I've just got that and the windows to do.

RAFTER. I thought all that would've been done by now.

MOFFAT. I thought so myself.

RAFTER. Why's it not then?

MOFFAT. 'Cos I've been needing a new bit brace and bevel. I should've gone over for them before, I know. (*Putting down his tools.*) But the boat's in now you said?

RAFTER. What are you doing?

MOFFAT. I'll walk down with you and go over for them this evening.

RAFTER. You can't go over Moffat.

MOFFAT. The house can wait a day.

RAFTER. It can't wait. You know as well as me we're expecting a man here. We've known for some time he's coming, now he's due. (*Beat.*) You can send Agnes over for your tools.

MOFFAT. Agnes?

RAFTER. Get on with something else in the meantime.

MOFFAT. Agnes is a child Rafter.

RAFTER. She's old enough to do her bit.

MOFFAT. She's never been over before. (*Making to go.*) She's not going to start now either.

RAFTER. You promised me Moffat, wait there a minute, you promised me, remember, and through me you promised Sinclair that there'd be a home here for him when he arrives.

MOFFAT. It's not just for me to make the man a home Rafter.

RAFTER. No one said it was.

MOFFAT. You see to getting the rest of the place in order then.

RAFTER. I've been seeing to nothing else. (*Beat.*) But you gave your word a house would be ready here.

MOFFAT. I know what I said.

RAFTER. That was your word, not mine. You're for ever reminding everyone in the town as well, especially me, how they're nothing without their word. Is yours not worth something any more?

MOFFAT. You know fine well it is.

RAFTER. Let's talk no more about changing it then. (*Beat.*) I'll see you and Agnes at the pier.

Blackout.

2.

A field.

An old tree at the back centre of stage.

Low light from stage right as of the sun beginning to set.

Suggestion of a few ploughed ridges from left to right, covering no more than a quarter of the stage, placed towards the front.

MARY GEAR *stands stage left. She looks at the ridges, at the sun, at the tree, and back again at the ridges. She indicates nothing.*

JOHN GEAR *approaches from stage right, pulling a cart, a shovel on it.*

JOHN. Wha' are you doing at the field Mary?

MARY (*still looking at the ridges*). Rafter wants us.

JOHN (*taking the spade down from the cart*). Tell him I've ploughed his field aw'ready. When the horse was grazin' I put his sheep t' nearer pasture. I stacked his grain after that.

MARY. He wants us t' get Sinclair's furniture from the pier.

JOHN (*uncomplaining*). I was about t' plough our field here.

MARY (*pointing*). Who's done tha' aw'ready?

JOHN. I made tha' start.

MARY. This morning?

JOHN. Aye, this mornin'. An' I was away for the horse t' carry on before the sun's down.

MARY. T' carry on like that?

JOHN (*putting the spade back on the cart*). Aye.

MARY. Wi' those ridges from east t' west?

JOHN. If that's wha' they are.

MARY. Am I ever goin' to get a break from these habits o' yours John?

JOHN. What habits are they Mary?

MARY. The ones I'm always up against.

JOHN. Eh?

MARY. The ones as regular as the sun there, as hard t' reach in aw'. (*Beat, rhetorical.*) Wha' d'you think I've been doin' aw' day?

JOHN. You've been makin' yer cloth Mary.

MARY. No John. I've been in the back o' some damp shed, sorting seed potatoes int' chunks, layin' them out for plantin'.

JOHN. They'll get planted the 'morrow then.

MARY. No when yer about t' waste the bit o' grace we get from the land.

JOHN. Waste how?

MARY. You must be a real idiot John.

JOHN. I'm no idiot Mary.

MARY. I swear you are.

JOHN. I'm tellin' you I'm no.

MARY. If I drew a horse I'd have to write underneath 'This is a horse' each time 'cos you are. 'Cos you can't tell what's what w'out it being pointed out. So I'll point this out for you again. (*Pointing.*) That's the sun there.

JOHN. Well done Mary.

MARY. It travels from east t' west, same as yer shafts and furrows.

JOHN. Does it now?

MARY. Aye. (*Beat.*) An' see the old tree there?

JOHN (*sarcastically*). Yer tellin' me there's a tree there in aw'?

MARY (*with mounting frustration*). I'm telling you it's t' the north John. That everything down from it – here, us, our patch o' land – all that's t' the south.

JOHN. Ta very much Mary, but I'm aware o' that.

MARY (*with a surge of impatience*). If you're aware o' it why don't your ridges go from north t' south then, t' that tree an' back? So both sides get what sunlight there is this summer. One side in the morning, the other after noon. So everythin' that's planted'll grow. So our field'll be bright, our crop whole.

JOHN. Aw' right Mary.

MARY. We might be better off for it in aw'.

JOHN. I'll do it like tha' after then.

MARY. You'll do it now.

JOHN (*taking the cart*). I'll do it when I'm done w' Rafter.

MARY. Rafter can wait.

JOHN. Aye, an' Sinclair's furniture?

MARY. That in aw'.

JOHN. Who's an idiot now Mary!?

MARY. What?

JOHN (*he starts off*). No one's gonna be better off if I don't take care o' that.

MARY (*shouting after him*). But I want you t' take care o' markin' the turf here, no some things at the pier. So you mind which way our field's t' be ploughed.

JOHN (*from afar*). I'll mind that easy enough.

MARY. You never mind though John. (JOHN *almost gone and now quieter.*) If only you would. (*Looking woefully back at the ridges.*) I might spare a thought for better then.

Blackout.

3.

The pier.

Early evening.

The foot of the pier is front centre. A narrow plank, supported by poles, leads up offstage left to the unseen boat.

Around the foot of the pier are several boxes and items of furniture. The boxes and furniture are wrapped in plain paper and tied with string. Some of the items of furniture (those referred to), despite being wrapped, are recognisable by their shape.

AGNES LESLIE MOFFAT *stands midway up the pier, looking out to the sea.*

MOFFAT *enters from stage right a few moments later, carrying a small suitcase, and waits at the foot of the pier.*

MOFFAT. Does the wind feel stronger to you Agnes?

AGNES. There's no wind.

MOFFAT. There was a whistle in the rigging there.

AGNES. I didn't hear any whistle.

MOFFAT. You didn't?

AGNES. No.

MOFFAT. The air's still enough I suppose.

AGNES (*coming down the pier*). The boat seems ready as well.

MOFFAT (*feeling his pockets*). You've got the tool merchant's address then?

AGNES. It's in my pocket.

MOFFAT. And the money?

AGNES. The money's safe and everything.

MOFFAT. You're about ready yourself then. (*Beat.*) More ready than me I'd say!

AGNES. I still don't see why I have to go all the way out there though.

MOFFAT. You're going to help me.

AGNES. I'm not going for you, I'm going for the sake of some man none of us even know.

MOFFAT. It doesn't matter if you know him Agnes.

AGNES (*going to the items mentioned*). I might as well be going for this old bed here, these chairs, that desk and table. (*Beat.*) Does anyone know him?

MOFFAT. No one that's been here these years.

AGNES. He must be someone to Rafter though?

MOFFAT. I don't know what he is to Rafter.

AGNES. He must be important in some way. Or have influence. He must be someone to Rafter for sure, there's no other reason why I'd be going. (*As she sees* RAFTER *approaching from stage right, the* GEARS *behind.*) Just because Rafter says I have to.

RAFTER (*shouting back*). Get a move on, you two.

AGNES (*looking at the group approaching*). That's all any of us do.

MOFFAT. You're free to do what you want Agnes.

AGNES. We're only free till he wants something. Now he wants something from me.

RAFTER *enters.*

RAFTER. You both made it then.

MOFFAT. We did.

JOHN *and* MARY *now enter.* JOHN *pulls the cart.* MARY *follows a short way behind.*

JOHN (*respectful*). Aw' right James?

MOFFAT. John.

AGNES. Hello Mary.

MARY. Sweet little Agnes.

JOHN. Are they Sinclair's?

RAFTER. That's the lot.

JOHN. Le' me get them up then.

JOHN *starts to lift some boxes onto the cart.*

MARY. We'll no get aw' that up by night.

RAFTER. Maybe you can get up what you can.

AGNES. Do you know why Rafter's going to all this trouble over Sinclair Mary?

MARY. I've been askin' myself the same question Agnes.

AGNES (*indicating* RAFTER). He doesn't go to any trouble over us.

MARY (*laughing nervously*). Listen t' her!

AGNES. I don't know why I should risk my life for him either.

RAFTER. You should be grateful someone like Sinclair's coming Agnes.

MARY. Grateful for another drain an' burden?

RAFTER. Sinclair's coming to ease our burden Mary, not add to it.

MARY. He's goin' t' do that is he?!

JOHN. Everyone in town's saying he will.

MARY. Aye, an' you'll repeat anythin' Rafter says t' you.

JOHN. You know yerself James?

MOFFAT. I don't hear too much from the town I'm afraid John.

RAFTER. John's just saying what everyone else is hoping.

JOHN. It's no' only me Mary.

RAFTER. It is not.

JOHN. See.

RAFTER. We all muddy and scrape through here.

MARY. Some more than others.

RAFTER. Some complain about it more than others as well.

MARY. I've every right t' complain.

RAFTER. You'll complain even when a man's bringing a remedy to it all Mary. When people are hopeful of him, you'll leave his furniture exposed. This one here'd rather whinge about going a short way across the sea for him as well.

AGNES. I didn't say I wouldn't go.

RAFTER. I should go myself and leave yous in this miserable state of ours, you don't deserve to see it changed.

MOFFAT. You don't know any more about Sinclair than we do Rafter. Never mind knowing what changes he'll make.

RAFTER. I know what he's written.

MOFFAT. And what's that?

RAFTER. Others know as well.

MOFFAT. They know what's been written in a few letters.

RAFTER. If you came to the town meetings you'd know there's more than that.

MOFFAT (*dismissively*). I'd know the usual gossip.

RAFTER (*irritated*). There's no gossip here this time.

MOFFAT. There's never anything else.

RAFTER. There's the growing word, James Moffat, that Sinclair will improve our lot. Nearly everyone else has heard it. Bad mouth it if you want. (*Beat.*) But there's a world out there whether you're interested in it or not, that world's changing by the day. Some of it for the good, some for the bad. This kind man's coming and saying he's going to put us in reach with what's good about it. You should hear some of the things he's said! What ideas! He'll lift all of us up. Give us a bit of protection against what's bad about that world as well.

AGNES. What's bad about it?

RAFTER. You won't have to know what's bad about it Agnes. That's what I'm saying. Just imagine the ease and comfort of it all!

MOFFAT. You've made your point now Rafter.

RAFTER. I'm only trying to educate the girl.

MOFFAT. She can do without your kind of education. (*Going to her.*) You go or stay if you want Agnes, don't listen to him. But I hope if you do go it's 'cos you want to help Sinclair, for no other reason than that. Because that value's in your heart. It's in laws and religions, it's talked about all over the place as well, but it's nowhere if it's not in there. I hope it's in my heart. I brought you up trying to put it in yours.

AGNES. No one else is doing anything out of the goodness of their hearts.

MOFFAT (*standing up and stepping back*). Never mind about them.

AGNES. But why should I?

MOFFAT. Because it's the only reason you can be sure of Agnes.

The keeper's signal, a noise as of a horn, is heard.

JOHN. That's the keeper's signal there now.

RAFTER. We can hear it as well as you John.

JOHN. The weather's set fair.

MARY. They're about ready t' sail off in aw'.

RAFTER. Can't you be ready yourself Agnes? (*Beat.*) Get on that boat there for one of the reasons you've been given?

Blackout.

4.

The church.

Night.

A storm batters outside.

Sound of a bell as though buffeted by the wind.

MOFFAT, *his clothes wet, seemingly exhausted and worn out, kneels and prays.*

MOFFAT (*pause*). I haven't been under this roof for twelve years now. It's taken a night like this to bring me back. (*Pause.*) I used to kneel here. Strong in a faith that stopped me sinking too deep. I had humility as well, like a ballast, that stopped me rising too high. (*Pause.*) But that faith went. You took it right enough. The ballast with it. I don't even know who You are any more. I don't know how to speak to You either. I'm not a man of words. I work with wood. But the chair is in the wood like the word is in language. Both are given, not owned or invented by anyone. For my part I've always tried to bring out what lies within the things You've given. Each time I take a piece of wood and make something from it, when I make a chair, I'm trying to put Your wood to good use. Isn't that like putting words to good use in a prayer? The chair's also like a prayer then. Maybe a better prayer. It takes time and care to make. If one part fails, the whole collapses. A chair's not easily put together like everyday words, like some prayers. (*Pause.*) Take then this floor, that roof, twelve years' worth of chairs as real prayers. I made them and offer them to You. (*Calling out.*) Intervene. Boats are at sea tonight. Give them clear passage through the storm. Don't take my daughter from me too.

The sound of the storm pressing in.

Blackout.

5.

The shore by the dunes.

The morning after the storm.

Absolute silence, quiet and still after the storm.

Some large logs and sticks are scattered about the front stage.

Downstage, in the nearest front centre lies a body, partially concealed by a log, the head towards stage left, the feet to the right. The face is turned upstage, the body face down. It is naked except for some loose white, under trousers.

Silence continues.

JOHN *and* MARY GEAR *are then heard approaching from upstage right.*

What they refer to whilst off is unseen.

MARY (*off*). Oh John.

JOHN (*off*). I see.

MARY (*off*). The keeper's house.

JOHN (*off*). He's unroofed.

MARY (*off*). The devastation.

JOHN (*off*). His chimney.

MARY (*off*). It's torn off.

JOHN (*off*). The whole length o' it down.

MARY *crosses at the back of the stage as though heading off left.*

MARY. The field'll be flooded for sure.

JOHN (*off*). Aw' the bricks in a line.

MARY. Our seed 'tatoes out.

JOHN *coming on and going downstage a little.*

JOHN. There's branches blown t' the beach here in aw'.

MARY. Never mind about branches.

JOHN. Logs there Mary.

MARY. There's no time t' look.

JOHN. Somethin' else in aw'.

MARY (*heading off upstage left*). Get t' the field John.

JOHN. Wait Mary. On the shore there. There's somethin' else in aw'. Is that a man there?

MARY (*not hearing*). I'll see you at the field.

JOHN (*shouting*). But there's a man there Mary.

MARY. A what?

JOHN. A man's here.

MARY (*stopping*). A man?

JOHN. Aye.

She now goes towards JOHN.

MARY. On the beach?

JOHN. Just here.

MARY. Where?

JOHN. It's a young man Mary.

MARY. There?

JOHN. His arm's there.

MARY. That's a man John.

JOHN. A young man I've said.

MARY. Dear God.

JOHN. I know.

MARY. He must've been washed up by the storm.

Reaching the man, MARY *stands about the head,* JOHN *about the feet.*

JOHN. Thrown from a boat.

MARY. He might've been there aw' night.

JOHN. You think he's drowned?

MARY (*looking more closely*). He's no moving.

JOHN. Is he no breathing at all?

MARY. I can't see any.

JOHN. He must be drowned then?

MARY. I would think he was.

JOHN (*without irony*). The poor soul.

MARY. To be drowned and washed up here.

JOHN. Aye.

MARY. Here of aw' places.

Pause. They look, then walk around the body so that MARY *is now at the feet and* JOHN *about the head.*

JOHN. I wonder who he is?

MARY (*as though knowing*). D'you know who he is?

JOHN. You know?

MARY. Aye.

JOHN. Who?

MARY. I think it's him.

JOHN. Him?

MARY. Aye him.

JOHN. Who's him?

MARY. The man Rafter's expectin'.

JOHN. That's no him.

MARY. That's the one who was comin' t' save us.

JOHN. I'm tellin' you it's no.

MARY. A lot of good he's going t' do now.

JOHN. It's no him Mary.

MARY. How d'you know?

JOHN. He's no due yet. He's no as young as that either. Rafter's said Sinclair's an old fella, all withered and bearded like.

MARY. You don't think it's him then?

JOHN. I'm tellin' you it's no.

MARY. Who d'you think it is then?

JOHN. He could be anyone Mary.

MARY. Anyone?

JOHN (*going in to look more closely*). Anyone at aw'. (*Short pause.*) From whatever boat or coast. Been brought like this t' us in aw'. Aw' wasted. Only good for the grave. What a loss. (*Beat, backing off with surprise and concern.*) Oh Mary!

MARY. What?

JOHN. Did you no' see him move there?

MARY. No.

JOHN. I saw his back move.

MARY. I saw nothin'.

JOHN. His back moved.

MARY. He's drowned John.

JOHN. He's no dead at aw'.

JOHN *starts away from the body.*

MARY. Where are you goin'?

JOHN. I'm goin' to get Rafter.

MARY. Yer leavin' me here?

JOHN *heads off stage right.*

JOHN. I'll be right down.

MARY. What about the field though?

JOHN (*almost off*). I'm more worried about him Mary.

MARY (*shouting after JOHN as he goes*). For all the good that'll do . . . John? (*Pointing at the man without looking.*) He's hardly even breathin'. If he's even breathin' at aw. (*Looking down at the body.*) I don't have time t' watch him. (*Looking back in the direction of the field.*) I've t' see the field. Check the seed 'tatoes. Get on w' the cloth. John should be seeing t' the sheep for tha'. No running up t' the square after you. 'Cos he thinks he saw you breathin'. (*Looking more closely herself.*) Oh you. Wha' did he even see at aw'. (*Pause.*) Is that breathin' there!

MOFFAT (*off*). Mary?

MARY. Who's that?

MOFFAT *enters stage left in a state of heightened distress, half-crazed, unseeing, not noticing the found man.*

MOFFAT. Is that you Mary?

MARY (*now concerned about the man*). It's you James.

MOFFAT (*approaching*). I've been all over the place.

MARY. Have you been here?

MOFFAT. I've been up and down the coast and there's nothing.

MARY. Nothin'?

MOFFAT. Agnes is nowhere.

MARY. There's a man here though.

MOFFAT. But Agnes is nowhere.

MARY. But look here.

MOFFAT (*hardly hearing*). There were waves over the dunes last night. Putting stones in the field, kelp in the grass, there's even a keel on the road.

MARY. What road?

MOFFAT. The road just there. What kind of wave lifts a keel up to there Mary? Breaks a boat like that with Agnes at sea?

MARY. Her boat wasn't back?

MOFFAT. I was up and down the coast all night I'm saying. Then I was in the church as it was battered. No boat came back.

MARY. They must've made it over then.

MOFFAT. Not on that sea.

MARY. That boat's over aw' the time.

MOFFAT. No boat's come back from that sea Mary. Only a keel beyond the dunes. That's all that's been brought back from that sea.

MARY. He's been brought in aw'.

MOFFAT. Eh?

MARY. This man here's been brought in aw'.

MOFFAT *looks down at the man, standing at his feet, as does* MARY, *standing about his head. The man simply serves to remind him more urgently of* AGNES' *possible fate.*

MOFFAT. Oh dear God.

MARY. I know.

MOFFAT. Oh Mary.

MARY. I thought he was drowned in aw'.

MOFFAT. Drowned?

MARY. It's aw' right though James.

MOFFAT. It's not alright. How can you say it's alright?

MARY. Say wha?

MOFFAT. Agnes might be lying somewhere.

MARY. Agnes?

MOFFAT. Her body. Her young self. Lying somewhere like this.

MARY. No sweet Agnes.

MOFFAT (*starting to go*). I have to see Rafter.

MARY. Wait a minute though James.

MOFFAT. I've to see him about Agnes.

MARY. Watch him a while w' me.

MOFFAT. I've my own concerns right now Mary.

MARY. You can't walk away and leave us here though.

MOFFAT. Have you not been listening or is the storm still ringing in your ears? Agnes is lost, she's my only concern right now, not some man you've found.

MARY (*shouting after him as he goes*). We've all got concerns Moffat. No just you. This man here's no just my concern either. There's a man here James.

MARY *looks as* MOFFAT *now goes, then back down at the body.*

MARY (*now with sympathy*). Some kind o' man he is in aw'. Just look at you. Yer more a woman or a boy. (*Short pause.*) You could even be a piece o' cloth. (*Her voice softening.*) Lyin' like tha'. (*Short pause.*) Yer arm aw' twisted an' wrung-looking. Maybe you've been made from some yarn yerself. A piece of cloth. Spun t' thread an' woven. (*Pause.*) Yer soft lookin' like my cloth in aw'. (*She now goes towards the body.*) Maybe you've been kneaded soft by a cloth-maker's hands. Kneaded as soft as cloth. What a rare thing that would be. (*Beat as she reaches out to touch him.*) I wonder, tell me, are you as soft as aw' that?

She touches his face, her hand moves onto his shoulder.

Blackout.

6.

A study.

A book-stand supports a thick book on a large desk (front stage right). Other books are on the desk. Behind the desk, at the back of the stage, is a window. A door down stage left.

RAFTER *sits at the desk.*

JOHN *stands in front of the desk, as though just arrived, next to a chair.*

RAFTER (*sharp and suspecting*). What do you mean you've found a man?

JOHN. A young man.

RAFTER. You don't just find someone John.

JOHN (*pointing off left*). He's down by the shoals.

RAFTER (*dismissing him*). Don't you think I've enough to contend with this morning? Haven't you seen the place? Get away with your nonsense, I've real problems here.

JOHN. Mary's w' him now though.

RAFTER. Mary's seen him too?

JOHN. Aye.

RAFTER. Why didn't you say?

JOHN. She's by the shoals in aw'.

RAFTER. A young man?

JOHN. Aye. Lying just over the dunes there.

RAFTER *gets up and goes towards the window at the back of the room.*

RAFTER. Did he say what he wants?

JOHN. He wasn't movin'.

RAFTER. He's dead then?

JOHN. I don't know.

RAFTER. Did you not feel for a pulse?

JOHN. I didn't touch any part o' him.

RAFTER. What about Mary?

JOHN. Her neither.

RAFTER. What have you done with him then?

JOHN. We've no done anythin'.

RAFTER. Did you not even see if there was something to identify him?

JOHN. Like what?

RAFTER (*disbelief*). You've just found a man John!

JOHN. Aye.

RAFTER. An' you didn't look if there was a piece of paper near him?

JOHN. I didn't see anythin' like tha'.

RAFTER. A bag or a chain?

JOHN. No.

RAFTER. What about something on him?

JOHN. He just had a rag on him.

RAFTER. There was no mark or scab?

JOHN. No tha' I saw.

RAFTER. A rash or sore even?

JOHN. Nothin' like that either.

RAFTER. I can't believe you saw no sign to tell us anything. People don't just appear from nowhere John, not without cause or reason. There's always a reason. We're supposed to find it. That's how we understand and know about things. That's how there's harmony.

There is a knock on the door and MOFFAT *enters.*

JOHN *remains by the desk,* MOFFAT *at the door, whilst* RAFTER *stands between.*

MOFFAT. Rafter?

RAFTER. Who's that?

MOFFAT. It's me.

RAFTER. I'm with John right now.

MOFFAT. I need your help.

RAFTER. I'm busy helping John.

MOFFAT. But I need to see about Agnes.

JOHN. What about Agnes?

MOFFAT (*to* JOHN). She was at sea last night.

JOHN. She would've still been on tha' boat?

MOFFAT (*to* RAFTER). I need to see if she got across.

JOHN. On tha' sea?

RAFTER. How am I expected to help you with that?

MOFFAT. However you can Rafter. The same way everyone here's always running about helping you however they can.

RAFTER. What has anyone here ever done for me?

MOFFAT. This man's for ever at your call.

RAFTER. For which he's lent a field.

MOFFAT. Was I lent a field for building that stand there?

RAFTER. Even so.

MOFFAT. I built it to hold these books of yours, 'books of great understanding, beauty and knowledge'. That's what you call them?

RAFTER. That is what I call them.

MOFFAT. You say they make you finer for reading them as well. But your neck was hurting. I built that stand to help you read. So you wouldn't have pain. Have you pain any more?

RAFTER. I haven't.

MOFFAT. And you can read?

RAFTER. When I get the chance.

MOFFAT. But are you finer for it? Have you ever seen that he is, John? (*A final cry.*) Show us that you are 'cos I've pain now.

RAFTER. John?

JOHN. Aye?

Ushering JOHN *out, talking privately to him.*

RAFTER. Get yourself back down to the beach and take that man to your barn.

JOHN. My barn?

RAFTER. Lock him there for now.

JOHN. Lock him for what?

RAFTER. Lock him there till we can learn something about him.

JOHN. Will I give him some straw at least?

RAFTER (*turning back to* MOFFAT). It's your straw John, give him as much as you want. (JOHN *goes*, RAFTER *shouts after him.*) Then get down to the pier. I heard Sinclair's furniture's been scattered about there. (*Beat.*) Now James?

RAFTER *closes the door behind him.*

MOFFAT (*sitting, as though drained*). I want to take a boat over Rafter.

RAFTER. I thought as much.

MOFFAT. A couple of fishermen to sail it as well.

RAFTER. Didn't you see the fishermen in the doorway there?

MOFFAT. I passed them.

RAFTER. If you'd stopped they would've told you their boats are wrecked.

MOFFAT. Not all of them.

RAFTER. The pier's smashed to bits James.

MOFFAT. There's other boats along the coast.

RAFTER. You think you'll find favours there?

MOFFAT. I can't sit about doing nothing.

RAFTER. I can't make a boat appear for you either James.

MOFFAT. You made Agnes go easily enough.

RAFTER. Now then. No. You know I didn't.

MOFFAT. She went at your request.

RAFTER. Agnes went of her own choice.

MOFFAT. With your persuasion.

RAFTER. I hope it was with your persuasion more than mine. You gave her the better reason.

MOFFAT. That's not true.

RAFTER. It was your words that seemed to turn her.

MOFFAT (*helplessly*). She didn't go because of me though.

RAFTER (*gently*). No one's accusing you James. Just don't go around accusing me's all I'm saying. That storm was general last night. No one's responsible. There would've been many boats at sea. We don't know how many have been destroyed, how many houses brought down, what coasts and harbours covered with wrecks. But we do know the next boat's due tomorrow. We know that and I give you all my prayers that Agnes will be on it.

MOFFAT (*quietly*). You might as well save your prayers Rafter.

RAFTER. There's nothing else we can do till then but pray and work.

MOFFAT. I know well enough the result of prayers.

RAFTER (*with feeling*). Then turn to work James. There's help to be had there. Lord knows there's enough to be done here now. (*Beat.*) How about getting yourself up to the new house an' seeing it's alright there for starters?

MOFFAT. I couldn't go near that house right now Rafter.

RAFTER. You'd be saving me the trouble to check it if you did, easing your own worries as well.

MOFFAT. I can think of better work for that.

MOFFAT *goes.*

RAFTER. What better work can there be than that Moffat? Especially now. Nothing will help us more than that.

Blackout.

7.

The town square.

A clock, reading 10.30, is hung from the wall on stage left.

Outside of RAFTER*'s house on the right. A few stairs leading up to the front door. A simple bench (a plank of wood supported by two stones either end) outside of the house. A few posters with small text to the effect of 'Sinclair arriving Sunday. Everyone to be at the Pier by Ten'.*

MARY *comes on stage left, nervously, heading towards the centre.*

MARY. John? Are you still here John? Where are you when I need you? John?

She sits down on the bench. Waits.

What am I goin' t' do now?

Looks at the clock.

JOHN *then enters.*

JOHN. Mary?

MARY (*getting up*). John.

JOHN. Yer here.

MARY. Where were you?

JOHN. I went for the cart.

MARY. You were supposed t' come straight t' the beach.

JOHN. I've just been there.

MARY. You've seen them?

JOHN. I saw.

MARY. I came runnin' up here.

JOHN. Where's he gone?

MARY. He just went.

JOHN (*going to* RAFTER*'s door*). I thought somethin' had happened t' you.

MARY. I got such a scare John.

JOHN. Yer aw' right though?

MARY. What are you doin'?

JOHN (*knocking*). Rafter?

MARY. Wait a minute John.

JOHN (*harder*). I have t' tell Rafter.

MARY. John.

JOHN (*stopping and turning to* MARY). What?

MARY. Don't.

RAFTER *enters.* MARY *steps back.*

RAFTER. What's this racket John?

JOHN. Eh?

MARY (*stepping back and sotto voce*). Just be quiet.

RAFTER. What's all this banging about?

JOHN (*apprehensively*). The man's gone.

RAFTER. Gone?

JOHN (*glancing back to* MARY). Aye.

RAFTER. I told you to put him in your barn.

JOHN. He was aw'ready gone from the beach though.

RAFTER. You told me she was watching him.

JOHN. She was watchin' him.

RAFTER. What are you doing in the square then Mary?

MARY (*nervously*). 'Cos he's no on the beach no more.

RAFTER. Where is he if he's not on the beach?

MARY. He ran off.

RAFTER. He was near death John said.

JOHN. So he was.

MARY. He woke though.

RAFTER. And ran off to where?

MARY (*pointing*). To the hills near the new house there.

RAFTER (*stepping to front stage*). What's he run up there for?

They head towards the front of stage and look off as though at the house on the hill.

JOHN. There's some kind o' mist there.

Bells have begun to ring.

RAFTER (*turning*). Mist?

JOHN. That looks too thick to be mist though.

RAFTER. Is that smoke?

MARY. It's not smoke.

RAFTER. The town's seen it's smoke as well as you Mary.

JOHN. Is the new house on fire?

MARY. It can't be on fire.

RAFTER. There's nothing else there but a house and wood. What else would be on fire? (*Now turning on her.*) Have you let some man up there to light it?

MARY. I didn't let him.

RAFTER. You couldn't watch him for five minutes?

MARY. I was watchin' him.

RAFTER. How's he there then?

MARY. I don't know.

RAFTER. He just rose from the dead?!

MARY. Aye.

RAFTER. Why?

MARY. I don't know, I said.

RAFTER. You must know something Mary, you were with him.

MARY (*trying to think of something*). Maybe I left him.

JOHN. You left him?

MARY (*back-pedalling*). Only for a while.

RAFTER. You left some strange man on his own?

MARY. I didn't see any harm.

All looking off downstage.

RAFTER (*pointing*). Can you see the harm now?

MARY. It's only a fire.

RAFTER (*hopeless*). It's in Sinclair's house Mary.

MARY. At least the town'll get t' it.

RAFTER. They won't get to it.

MARY. You don't know that.

RAFTER. It's too far up for them to get to.

JOHN. It's just going to burn?

RAFTER. To the ground John.

JOHN. Aw' t' ashes?

RAFTER. After our preparations there's nothing we can do but watch it all burn.

Short pause whilst they all look at the fire.

JOHN. Why would the man light a fire up there anyway?

RAFTER. God alone knows why John.

JOHN. He was probably cold.

RAFTER. Cold?

JOHN. Did you see if he was cold?

MARY. How would I see?

JOHN. There's no other reason for a small fire takin' over. (*Innocently.*) Look at the size o' it now, it's lighting up the hill.

RAFTER (*beginning to realise*). Dear God alive John.

JOHN. You'll be able to see that for miles.

RAFTER. It's a fire on a hill.

JOHN. It's like some beacon.

RAFTER. I asked if there was a sign as well.

MARY. A sign for what?

RAFTER. For some kind of sign Mary. (*Taking a step downstage and with each sentence his certainty grows.*) An' it's a fire on a hill. Staring us in the face all the time. Could there be a clearer sign than that? A fire on a hill's a signal. (*Generally, with force and conclusive finality.*) He's run up there to send a signal.

MARY. A signal t' who?

RAFTER (*filling with panic*). How would I know who? To the others.

JOHN. Wha' others?

RAFTER. I didn't even think to ask if there might be others.

MARY. There's no others.

RAFTER. There'll be others related to him.

JOHN. I thought he was some innocent from a boat.

RAFTER. What's innocent about a boat being near here John? Where do you think we're living? What world do you think this is? (*As though seeing.*) They've probably got six boats or more now, lining the shore.

JOHN. Comin' towards us?

RAFTER. An outside threat's coming towards us for sure.

MARY (*her fear growing*). That's no what that is.

RAFTER (*floundering around*). They'll be heading for the shore house now because of it Mary. Killing the keeper, hanging his old chicken neck from a staff. Then they'll be up to town before we know it, taking over our homes, our goods, our women too.

JOHN. Our women?

RAFTER. They won't even care for women – children either – coming up on us like this. Insinuating themselves with their evil. Their hate. They'll take care of the women after they've knelt our men in a line.

MARY. For wha'?

RAFTER. To execute every last one of them.

JOHN. That young man we found?

RAFTER. In the back of the head.

MARY (*fearfully*). He's come to kill us?

RAFTER. Bury the lot of us Mary. (*Wildly accusing.*) An' you might as well have pulled the trigger yourself.

MARY (*no longer defiant*). Not me.

RAFTER (*grabbing and turning her to face the fire*). You just had watch him.

MARY. It's no my fault though.

RAFTER (*still holding her violently by the arm*). You might as well have taken him up there by the hand.

MARY. You can't blame me.

RAFTER. Helped him light his signal for all to see. (*Throwing her off.*) You've ruined us.

MARY. Stop shoutin' at me.

RAFTER. Destroyed each one of us.

MARY (*pointing to the fire*). You should be shoutin' at him. No me. See wha' he's done there.

RAFTER. I see all too clear.

MARY (*pointing to her chest*). Bloody ask what else he might've done here then.

RAFTER. Here?

MARY. What else he might've done to me.

JOHN. To you?

RAFTER (*dismissively*). He's done nothing to you.

MARY (*starting to cry*). You don't even care what's been done t' me.

JOHN. I care Mary.

MARY (*with real hurt and anger*). You left me on my own w' him John. He just cares about blamin' me for tha'. I came runnin' up here an' none of you even asked what tha' man's done to me.

Blackout.

8.

A workshop.

A door in the centre.

MOFFAT *roughs a plank of wood. Other planks of wood are stacked against the inside wall.*

He is closed in.

JOHN *arrives and knocks hard on the door.*

JOHN. James? Open yer door. James?

JOHN *listens at the door whilst* MOFFAT *waits, hoping* JOHN *will go away.*

I know yer there. (*He knocks again, harder still.*) James?

MOFFAT. Get away John.

JOHN. You've t' come t' town.

MOFFAT (*continuing to work*). I'm not coming anywhere.

JOHN. There's some fury in the town.

MOFFAT. There's always something with that lot.

JOHN. There's a fire in the house you've built.

MOFFAT. There's no such thing.

JOHN. The man we found's burnt it t' nothin'.

MOFFAT. Him?

JOHN. Open the door.

MOFFAT. I'm opening it.

JOHN. Rafter's sayin' there's others comin' in aw'.

MOFFAT. Others?

JOHN. Hundred's o' them.

MOFFAT. Hold on a minute.

JOHN. An' what this one's aw'ready done t' Mary.

MOFFAT *now opens the door.*

MOFFAT. To Mary?

JOHN. Oh James.

MOFFAT (*with concern*). What's he done to Mary?

JOHN. He's sprung up like some animal an' raped her.

MOFFAT. Your Mary?

JOHN. Aye, my Mary. Now he's loose t' wreak havoc. We need everyone out w' pitch forks an' guns, searchin' barns an' stores. You've t' help find him.

MOFFAT. I can't do that.

JOHN. Did you no hear me right?

MOFFAT. I've work to get done John.

JOHN. It's no work we need now.

MOFFAT. I've wood to bend, a keel to collect from the dunes.

JOHN. A keel?

MOFFAT. An old keel to build a boat around.

JOHN. Where are you goin' on a boat James?

MOFFAT. I'm away to find Agnes John.

JOHN. Yer no goin' anywhere w' what's happenin' here.

MOFFAT. There's things happening to me as well John.

JOHN. Aye. I know. But they're no just happenin' t' you. Wake up man. There's things happenin' t' us aw' t'gether.

MOFFAT. We're never together.

JOHN. We're t'gether now.

MOFFAT. You've no need for me then with the town on side. Be glad you've got that. (*Starting to close the door with resolve.*) There was no help for me when I asked.

JOHN. You never asked me though.

MOFFAT. I'm better off on my own.

JOHN (*stopping it*). No one's better like tha'.

MOFFAT (*forcing it closed*). Quit pestering me John.

JOHN. Don't close yer door on me.

MOFFAT. Just get away now.

JOHN. James? Open yer door. (*He knocks hard.*) James?

MOFFAT *waits for* JOHN *to go away.*

I know yer there. (*Beat.*) James?

JOHN *then knocks again, more weakly, as he realises his isolation.*

Keep yer door closed then. Don't bother what's been done here. Against Mary or me. I'll find the man myself. Shiverin' in some burn, tremblin' in a byre. (*His anger growing.*) An' when I do I'll ravage him, cleanse the place o' those w' him in aw'. But before I do they better get t' you first, hidin' out here. You coward. (*Hopelessly.*) I thought you'd look over us. (*With venom.*) Yer a piece o' scum. I hope they raze you t' the ground. Leave you as ashes. (*Beat.*) Yer as much t' me as him, James Moffat, an' belong t' this place as little.

Blackout.

9.

The town square at night.

The clock hangs broken, stopped at after twelve. The bench is upturned. Various objects litter the ground. Torn posters are cast around.

Long pause.

Some distant and intermittent sounds of a crowd rioting are heard.

RAFTER *exits his door, disturbed by the noise and looking to see its source.*

Pause.

MARY *enters running from stage right, out of breath, scared.*

She looks back as the sound seems to approach and grow louder.

RAFTER (*cautiously*). Is that them?

MARY. Tha's them.

RAFTER. Coming back through at this late hour.

MARY. They're at the top o' the town.

RAFTER. What a noise they're making.

RAFTER *comes away from his door.*

Look what they've done to the square as well.

MARY. They've done worse elsewhere.

RAFTER (*setting the bench straight*). They've already searched here though.

MARY. They're no lookin' no more.

RAFTER *stops moving the bench.*

RAFTER (*nervously*). That's the noise?

MARY. That's the cause o' it.

RAFTER. Where did they find him?

MARY. Near the house.

RAFTER (*with sudden activity*). We better open up the hall then.

MARY. The hall?

RAFTER. Get yourself there Mary and lay out some benches. He'll need to be questioned. I'll direct the crowd so we can hear him.

RAFTER *starts to head off stage right.*

MARY. Yer no goin' t' direct them anywhere.

RAFTER. We've process Mary.

MARY. It's too late for yer process. (RAFTER *stops as she speaks.*) John's aw'ready cut at the man's nose an' took pieces from 'is face.

RAFTER. I never told him to do that.

MARY. The fish knife's been 'round half the town at least. Did you tell them t' do that? Or drag the man through 'ere, t' break glass in his path, w' aw' the dogs followin'?

RAFTER. To drag him where?

MARY. Where do you think?

RAFTER. They can't do that either.

MARY. You don't know what they can do. You can only start them on it. I'm no havin' it on me. That's what you started.

RAFTER. What would be on you?

MARY. It's no on me I'm sayin'.

RAFTER. You've shame all over you Mary.

MAR (*aggressively*). The shame's on you.

RAFTER (*stepping back*). I never told anyone to hurt him.

MARY. You put a fear into them Rafter. A panic into me 'cos you panicked.

RAFTER (*defensively*). I never panicked either.

MARY. You said thousands were comin' for us.

RAFTER. I put men on the shore for that Mary.

MARY. W' sticks on their shoulders!?

RAFTER (*hollowly*). The sight of them would've driven any threat away I'm saying.

MARY. But there was no threat. Only one man came. (*Pointing off.*) Was he that threat?

RAFTER. I'm not the one to be questioned here Mary!

MARY (*unrelenting*). He was never a question.

RAFTER. That's enough now.

MARY. A man's at least a question. You can't just say who someone is. Make up wha' they are. How could you say those things?

RAFTER. 'Cos those things happen.

MARY. They weren't happenin' here though.

RAFTER (*showing his vulnerability and fear*). You don't know what was about to happen here. You don't know the terrible things that happen – whole peoples get slaughtered. I thought that was going to happen here.

MARY. But you were mistaken Rafter.

RAFTER. We might've been wiped out.

MARY. Admit to them you were mistaken.

RAFTER (*as though persuading himself*). I couldn't let them be wiped out Mary. That man was a menace. The others that were near were driven away. Those must be the facts. I'm no more mistaken about them than the fire. (*Beat.*) Was I mistaken about that?

MARY. By its meaning.

RAFTER. By the meaning of your accusation as well then?

MARY. By mine?

RAFTER (*recovering himself*). It gave them encouragement as much as me.

MARY. No.

RAFTER. Maybe you were mistaken? Is that what's on you? Comin' screaming in here. Tell me if it is. John too. They'll stop quick enough then. (*Now unrelenting himself.*) Were you mistaken?

MARY. Yer no making me decide.

RAFTER. I'm asking if you were mistaken, Mary Gear?

MARY. Only as much as you, Charles Rafter.

The offstage noise is now impending.

RAFTER (*understanding her*). Then neither of us were.

MARY. Neither of us?

RAFTER. That's right Mary. (*Hollowly stepping back.*) So they've been wound up fair enough.

JOHN *enters from stage left, oblivious to* RAFTER *and* MARY, *who, in turn, part to let* JOHN *enter between them. He enters back first as he is pulling a long rope. He is wet with sweat and blood. When* JOHN *is halfway onto the stage the scene ends without sight of the found man tied to the end of the rope.*

MARY (*looking off*). Dear God.

RAFTER. We've no need for the hall either.

MARY. My John.

RAFTER. Stand back yourself and let them unwind as they will.

Blackout.

10.

The shore by the dunes as in Scene 5.

Silence except for sound of sea and rain.

Some large logs and sticks remain scattered about the front of the stage.

We see from the back of the stage the faint light from a lantern as though floating.

The light approaches, we catch a glimpse of a figure, before it recedes.

AGNES (*very softly off*). Hello? Hello? Is someone here?

MOFFAT *struggles on stage as he heaves a keel. Only the front of the keel is visible front stage right. The keel barely moves.*

MOFFAT (*with built-up frustration*). Up. Get up now. I'll get you up. A keel's the backbone of a boat. My boat will have a good keel. This place is like a boat with a rotten keel, splintered and cracked and only fit for sinking.

The figure approaches again and becomes visible. The figure wears a pale dress and a shawl (different to the clothes she left wearing). As the figure nears we see that it is AGNES.

AGNES (*softly off*). Someone is there?

MOFFAT (*not hearing*). I'll put my faith in you.

AGNES (*off*). Who is it?

MOFFAT. Not anywhere else.

AGNES (*off*). Is that you Dad?

MOFFAT (*only hearing now, without looking*). Who's that?

AGNES (*louder, coming on*). Dad?

MOFFAT (*stopping*). Who's doing that I said?

AGNES. It's me Dad.

MOFFAT (*confused, looking about without seeing her*). 'Me'?

AGNES. Agnes.

MOFFAT. Agnes is away.

AGNES. I'm right here.

MOFFAT (*making out her figure*). Agnes is away I said.

AGNES. Oh Dad.

MOFFAT (*now seeing her*). You're here?

AGNES. I'm here.

MOFFAT (*overcome with joy*). You are here.

AGNES. Oh Dad.

MOFFAT (*holding her in front of him by her arms*). How did you get here?!

AGNES. I was found.

MOFFAT. By who?

AGNES. Some fishermen.

MOFFAT. I thought I'd lost you.

AGNES. I was in the sea.

MOFFAT. I couldn't lose you as well.

AGNES. I thought I was going to drown.

MOFFAT. But they pulled you from the sea?

AGNES. They brought me here.

MOFFAT (*standing back*). And put your feet on the ground, your little toes, like horseshoe crabs, back on the sand! All of you here! I thought you'd never be here again. (*Beat and going as though to look.*) Where are these wonderful men?

AGNES (*remaining*). They've turned right back.

MOFFAT. They'll stay and be thanked.

AGNES. They dropped me here and went.

MOFFAT (*shouting as he goes upstage*). Hello men?

AGNES. They didn't want to come ashore Dad. They weren't from near here. (*Pointing.*) They saw some trouble in the other bay and went.

MOFFAT. What trouble?

AGNES. By the pier.

MOFFAT. Is that another fire there?

AGNES. Everyone was there in a mob, shouting and holding torches.

MOFFAT. Everyone?

AGNES (*going a little towards him*). It looked like the town was lined up on the shore.

MOFFAT. They must all be gathered.

AGNES. Gathered for what though?

MOFFAT. John said something up at the house before, all sorts of confusion about some man they'd found.

AGNES. What man did they find?

MOFFAT (*awkwardly*). I don't really know, Agnes. I've been up at the house the whole time you've been away. I've heard nothing about him since either. (*Beat.*) I've no idea what's been happening here.

Blackout.

11.

The remains of the pier.

The foot of it is intact and some remaining supporting poles continue from that, receding to the furthest depth of upstage left.

The sound of the tide approaching rapidly. Rain continues.

Downstage, extreme left and right (the centre is clear), debris of the pier is scattered. A few planks of wood jutting at angles. Also, the half-submerged, half-broken remains of some of Sinclair's furniture lie about.

At the furthest pole the found man is tied. All that can be made out of him is that his skin is strikingly white and pale, his head slumped to the side, his arms bound by a rope at the elbows and tied behind the pole.

JOHN *is wet up to his waist and stands halfway upstage.* RAFTER *stands lower down at the left.* MARY *stands yet further down, a shadowy figure, bottom right. They all look outwards as the man begins to disappear.*

RAFTER. That's him then John?

JOHN. That's him.

RAFTER. You've tied him there?

JOHN. He's tied there.

   Pause.

RAFTER. The tide's some force tonight, isn't it?

JOHN. It's never raced in like tha' before.

RAFTER. It's nearly about his chest already.

JOHN. It was comin' in faster than I could run.

RAFTER. You would've tied him tight then I'd imagine?

JOHN. He won't be runnin' free again.

RAFTER (*betraying regret*). No, I don't suppose he will.

JOHN. You can be sure o' that.

RAFTER. We best be. Sure of that anyway. I'm not sure of much else concerning him.

JOHN. What more d'you need t' be sure o' Rafter?

RAFTER. Nothing John, ignore me. (*Short pause.*) I just meant we didn't learn that much reason for his being here, that's all. What can we even say about him? Only that he arrived naked and leaves us haggard. In the short time between we didn't manage much understanding, harmony either, amongst all the noise and commotion that was made.

The man has disappeared entirely.

JOHN. He won't be causin' any more now.

RAFTER. No, he won't be anyway John. (*Beat.*) I'll just leave you to wait if you don't mind. When the tide's out, cut him down, will you? Take him on your cart to some empty place and bury him there, leaving no trace or stone.

JOHN. I found him once, I'll bury him deep so he's never found again.

MOFFAT *enters with* AGNES, *downstage right.*

MOFFAT. What's going on here Mary?

MARY (*quietly and filled with sadness*). You've come here in aw' James.

AGNES (*following, looking about*). Is this the pier?

MOFFAT. The pier was here.

MARY. Agnes?

MOFFAT. Agnes said she saw some lights.

AGNES (*pointing off*). I saw those lights from the sea.

MARY. You were safe at sea aw' the time?

AGNES. I was brought in on this tide.

MOFFAT. What's this activity Mary?

MARY. It's 'cos we got that man.

AGNES (*to* MARY). Where is he?

MARY (*holding* AGNES *to her*). You don't want t' know, sweet Agnes.

MOFFAT (*already going towards*). Rafter?

RAFTER. What do you want Moffat?

MOFFAT. Mary said you've got that man.

JOHN. Mind yer business about him.

MOFFAT (*to* RAFTER). Did you get him or not I'm asking?

JOHN (*with emphasis*). I got him like I said.

MOFFAT. What have you done with him then?

RAFTER (*with discomfort*). He's been taken care of.

MOFFAT (*understanding immediately*). You're here for that?

JOHN. Tha's right.

MOFFAT (*pointing to the sea*). Is that your care out there John?

JOHN *stands silent.*

(*To* RAFTER.) That's your care there Rafter?

RAFTER *silent as well.*

Mary?

MARY. That's the end o' it anyway.

MOFFAT. You drowned him for starting some fire?

RAFTER. There were other reasons Moffat.

MOFFAT. What reasons?

RAFTER. This is not the time to discuss reasons.

JOHN. You already know what he did to Mary.

MOFFAT. You've put him there for that?

MARY (*solemnly*). You put him there as much as us James.

MOFFAT. I didn't do anything to him.

MARY. You wanted nothin' t' do w' him either.

MOFFAT. I was up at my house.

MARY. An' you walked over his head like it was a stone t' get there in aw'.

MOFFAT. With good reason.

MARY (*putting* AGNES *forward*). Your reason's here.

MOFFAT (*going to* AGNES). I had to get her back.

MARY. She's no back 'cos o' you.

MOFFAT. I didn't know that.

41

MARY. You knew about him though. You would've left him t' rot in the sea, be picked open by birds in aw'.

MOFFAT (*dropping back*). I left him there for worse.

MARY. Aye, you left him there for us.

JOHN. But we had reason Mary.

MARY. No John.

JOHN. Aye, we did.

RAFTER. We've been through this already Mary.

MARY. We had no right.

RAFTER. We did what we thought right at the time. Who can do more than that?

MARY. Take yer comfort there then.

RAFTER. Take some comfort there yourself Mary.

MARY (*on the verge of tears*). I'm no able.

JOHN. What's he sayin' Mary?

JOHN *passes between* MOFFAT *and* RAFTER *as he approaches* MARY. *They talk as though they are alone.*

MARY. He's sayin' the man didn't do anythin' t' me John.

JOHN (*more tearful than angry*). You said he touched you.

MARY. I'm the one who touched him.

JOHN. You?

MARY. Aye.

JOHN. For what?

MARY. I don't know, John.

JOHN. For what, Mary?

MARY. Just t' see.

JOHN. T' see what though?

MARY. T' see if he'd wake. I don't know. If he was breathing. He woke. But he hardly looked at me, never mind touched me. He hardly looked at anythin' here.

JOHN (*turning to anger*). He looked at me Mary.

MARY. Don't look at me like tha' John.

JOHN. You let 'im see me like it.

MARY. I know what he must've saw.

JOHN (*now as a scream*). Aye, me. Yer John's wha' he saw. (*Pointing to the sea.*) You caused aw' that? You? (*Beat.*) You shouldn't be seein' me yerself for causin' it'.

MARY (*pulling her shawl up*). Don't you think I know tha'?

JOHN. You shouldn't be seein' anythin' here Mary.

MARY. I know that as well as you.

JOHN. What are you still doin' here then? Get out o' my face. Get away from the lot o' us.

MARY *looks at everyone in silence, pulls the shawl over her head, then goes.*

Silence continues.

He did nothing t' her Rafter.

RAFTER (*weakly*). Don't forget what you've done for us though John.

JOHN (*going off in the opposite direction to* MARY). I'm away for the cart.

RAFTER (*emptily as* JOHN *goes off*). Our home's our own again. There'll be no more trouble in our lives either.

AGNES (*stepping forward, nervously*). But what trouble was there?

RAFTER (*tired*). Trouble that's no worry of yours Agnes.

MOFFAT. I'd like to know myself Rafter.

RAFTER (*impatiently*). You're not going to know.

AGNES. I don't understand what I've come back to though.

RAFTER (*with affection*). Just be glad you're back with us at all Agnes. (*To* MOFFAT.) You as well. You've got your happiness Moffat. Go home and come back early tomorrow, ready to join in with ours.

MOFFAT (*uncomprehending*). What happiness can you have here now?

RAFTER. We can try and put this behind us and turn our thoughts to Sinclair.

MOFFAT. Sinclair?

RAFTER (*deflated*). He's due this morning, remember. (*Pensively.*) It was all supposed to be in order now. How far from order we are? (*Beat.*) But the sun'll soon be up, there'll be a new day coming with it as well. (*About to go.*) Let's all rest in our beds a while before we meet to welcome Sinclair here.

MOFFAT. You still want to welcome him to this?

RAFTER. He for one will be spared knowing about it.

RAFTER *goes.*

MOFFAT (*sotto voce, looking about*). We can't welcome him to this.

AGNES. He'll go if he knows.

MOFFAT. We can't keep quiet about it Agnes.

AGNES (*remaining*). What did I risk my life for though if he'll just go? I didn't go out there for some bed, a table either.

MOFFAT. I hope you went for him Agnes.

AGNES. I didn't go for some stranger.

MOFFAT. What did you go for then?

AGNES. I don't want to lose out 'cos of what you've all done to one either.

MOFFAT. Agnes?

AGNES. I wanted to go for us.

MOFFAT. What do you mean, 'us' Agnes?

AGNES. For the difference Sinclair's going to make for the town. You said I was free to go 'cos I wanted to. That's the reason I went. (*Beat.*) Not to come back to worse.

Blackout.

12.

A field in the clear light of dawn.

Absolute quiet.

A strong and low light rises and streams in from stage left.

Indication of a few ploughed ridges from top to bottom lit by the sun.

MARY enters, despondent, wearing the same clothes, her shawl over her head. She carries a sack. She puts the sack down as she notices the ridges.

She looks at the ridges, at the sun, at the tree, and back again at the ridges. There seems to be a change, a slight lift, in her mood.

JOHN enters stage right with the cart. His shovel rests on the cart and, like MARY, he wears the same clothes.

He stops when he sees MARY. He looks at her silently for a moment whilst she continues to look down at the ridges.

JOHN. What are you here for Mary?

MARY. I brought the seed potatoes.

JOHN. Leave them there.

MARY. Are you no headin' t' the pier?

JOHN (*short*). What would I be doin' at the pier?

MARY (*submitting*). I don't know.

JOHN (*taking his spade*). This is the first chance I've had t' get here. I want t' do some ploughin'. I've brought Rafter's sheep from the nearer pasture. I stacked his grain again and moved his horse t' fresh grazin'. When the old mare's fed I'm goin' t' carry on moving our ridges.

MARY (*taking her shawl down*). When were these moved though?

JOHN. Before the storm.

MARY. You remembered?

JOHN. North to south.

MARY. You did mind.

JOHN. Aye, like you said, so I can be left t' plough myself.

MARY. You can't plough though John.

JOHN. Why no?

MARY. The ground's sodden.

JOHN. It's still sodden?

MARY. It's soaked.

JOHN. I'll sink t' my shin.

MARY. We've nought t' plant anyway.

JOHN. What about the seed potatoes?

As he takes one from the sack.

MARY. I had them chopped an' left out. (*Beat.*) They were left out in the wet too long. (*As he sees himself.*) They've turned.

JOHN. They're rank.

MARY. They've aw' split.

JOHN. The lot's rotten. That's no right Mary. (*Struggling to keep his tears back.*) I've been up aw' night, nickin' through lumps and stones, t' come back t' a sodden field an' rotten spuds.

MARY. Let's no bother about the field now John.

JOHN. It was goin' t' be ready though. I wanted it t' be ready in aw'. Now none of it's goin' t' b' ready. (*Recovering himself.*) Ach, at least somethin's in the ground 'cos these won't be.

MARY. Somethin' is in the ground John. Aye. It's cost us dear in aw'.

Pause, during which the keeper's signal is faintly heard in the distance. MARY *is alert to it and responds with an emerging optimism.*

But it doesn't have to cost us everythin' John.

JOHN. How's tha'?

MARY. That's the keeper's signal there.

JOHN. I know what it is.

MARY. Sinclair comin' now. Maybe we've a new chance with his coming?

JOHN. A chance for what?

MARY. A chance t' be better John, better t' him, t' anyone in aw'. We can be like these ridges, ploughed in the field. Before they went one way, now they go another. You moved them. Even though the sun's fixed an' habits are hard, they were moved. (*Trying to smile*.) Can't we be moved in aw'? Where we've been wrong we can be shifted and put right. Just the same way a useless field, growin' only half a crop, can be turned an' made full, can't we be turned an' made better ourselves?

JOHN. But I try my best aw'ready Mary.

MARY. I know you do.

JOHN. What've I done that I need t' be better then?

MARY. Oh John.

JOHN. I work hard.

MARY. You do.

JOHN. I do what has t' be done.

MARY. That's right.

JOHN. I do what I'm told.

MARY. It's no you.

JOHN. I believe what I'm told in aw'. That is my best Mary. An' where does it get me? What gets done for aw' that? (*Short pause*.) This field's been ruined 'cos o' one man. (JOHN *packs up his spade, lifts the sack onto the cart*.) Go meet Sinclair if you want. But I'm doin' nothing for no other man again.

JOHN *starts to go.*

MARY (*tenderly*). Won't you do it for me though John? Come to the pier? (JOHN *almost gone*.) If only you would. (*Looking back briefly at the ridges*.) So we don't have t' be ruined in aw'.

Blackout.

13.

A clearing.

A bright and clear morning.

The sound of bells ringing in the distance as though in celebration.

An indication of the base of the original door frame, some planks of wood stacked, in an otherwise empty space.

MOFFAT *finishes clearing the remaining ashes into a pile stage left.*

RAFTER *enters from the back, short of breath but his energy recovered, dressed in a suit.*

RAFTER. Good day to you Moffat.

MOFFAT. Catch your breath Rafter.

RAFTER. Making me run up here!

MOFFAT. There was no need to run.

RAFTER. I've come from the pier.

MOFFAT. Has the boat come in?

RAFTER. You were supposed to be there.

MOFFAT. Sinclair's arrived?

RAFTER. He's on his way up now.

MOFFAT. You better get back down to meet him then.

RAFTER (*going upstage a little*). The whole town but you's meeting him. That's the workers there, leaving the fields. The cloth's folded away. The children are out of school as well.

MOFFAT (*going up a little*). Is that Mary there?

RAFTER. Even Mary's come to bring him here.

MARY *enters, also out of breath, now changed out her working clothes and wearing a dress.*

MARY (*sheepish*). Hello James.

MOFFAT. Mary.

RAFTER (*anxious*). Where are they now?

MARY. Coming along the path by the bays.

RAFTER (*briefly going up to look*). Already?

MARY. They're nearly at the cusp. (*To* MOFFAT.) John's no come up has he?

MOFFAT. He's got more manners than to show his face here.

MARY (*nervously, innocently*). I just want t' welcome Sinclair t' his new home James.

RAFTER. That's what everyone wants.

MOFFAT. There's no kind of home for anyone in this place Rafter. (*Beat.*) The minute Sinclair gets here I'll tell him as much myself.

MARY. Tell him wha'?

MOFFAT. I won't build till I've spoken about that man Mary.

RAFTER. You'll say nothing about him to Sinclair.

MOFFAT. I won't misuse my words any more than the wood Rafter.

RAFTER. You'll keep your mouth shut like the rest of us Moffat.

MOFFAT (*categorically*). Not when we've promised Sinclair a home. I gave my word to build one, you reminded me of that promise as well. But if I was to cut any wood now it wouldn't be a home I'd be building with it. He's not reached a home, he's not going to reach one either till the whole town makes one here first.

MARY (*with worry also*). You never want anythin' t' do w' the town.

MOFFAT. I'm talking about the town now.

RAFTER. You stepped out of our affairs a long time ago.

MOFFAT. That may be so.

RAFTER (*with growing fury*). You're not stepping back in now.

MOFFAT. Others will want to stand with me.

RAFTER. You've no ground with the people here.

MARY. Yer no someone t' tell me or them how t' make anything either.

MOFFAT. We've failed someone Mary. I've failed him myself. I'm not going to stand here to fail him or myself again. (*Insistent with force.*) I won't live with my head down.

RAFTER (*equally*). You'd rather bring all of us down?

MOFFAT. We couldn't be down any more.

RAFTER. You're determined to keep us there as well.

MOFFAT (*accusing with all his anger*). You keep us there Rafter. Ready to welcome one man after treating another like nothing. Now you want to forget he ever lived. 'Cos you think we might go forward with Sinclair? To some world out there? You're ignorant of everything in the world if you think there's any going forward like that.

RAFTER (*challenging*). But we've already lost our chance with the man we found. He might've been saved but he wasn't. He might've made a difference to our lives as well. But he's not going to be saved now. (*Frantically pointing.*) We've only Sinclair to look to.

MOFFAT (*almost appealing*). We can look to ourselves Rafter. Can we not start by looking there?

MARY (*anxiously*). Sinclair's just over the cusp aw'ready James.

MOFFAT (*defiant*). I'll keep him walking any further then.

MARY. That's John there w' him in aw'. He's dressed in his best! Comin' in aw'! (*Beat.*) Don't punish John along w' me James.

They go as though to look down at the approaching procession.

RAFTER. He'd sooner punish the lot of us.

MARY (*her hopes rising up in spite of herself*). Can't you forgive us instead? The same way John's forgiven me.

RAFTER (*remaining aggressive*). Half of them didn't even see that man.

MARY. They've only the best intentions.

RAFTER. You want to punish them as well?

MOFFAT. What about the other half of them?

MARY. I don't know about them James. But I know about myself, that's what you were sayin'. An I've only the best of hopes in my head now, believe me, John too, hopes as solid as the old tree in the back o' our field.

RAFTER. Agnes told me she's hopes of her own.

MOFFAT. Agnes is there too.

RAFTER. She was waiting before anyone at the pier.

MARY. Now she's running ahead o' them aw'.

RAFTER. You won't even build and lose your precious word for her?

MOFFAT. For Agnes?

RAFTER. Give up yours so she can discover the worth of Sinclair's.

MOFFAT (*insistent*). What will I be without my word though?

MARY. There can't be any blame losin' it for the love of her. (*Beat.*) Have you no done enough for that reason aw'ready?

MOFFAT (*helplessly*). What else could I do Mary? (*Beat.*) She's only a child.

RAFTER *and* MOFFAT *look upstage as* JOHN, *then* AGNES *enter.* JOHN *is now dressed in a suit. They stop the moment* RAFTER *finishes speaking as* AGNES *turns to welcome the imminent Sinclair. Sound of bells and celebration grows.*

RAFTER (*with urgency*). Take a step forward for her now then.

MARY. She's coming up the path.

RAFTER. She was lucky enough to be saved James.

MARY (*going towards* JOHN). Let us aw' be so lucky.

RAFTER. That's right. Don't let these days be for nothing. Bear what you've done in silence, we'll all bear it with you if it helps. Take a step forward now, smile and clap. You're not really going to deny Sinclair a little peace, have us lose out and be without some hope ourselves, come on now, is that to be our condition just because of some man we found?

Blackout.

End.

A Note Concerning the Period

The objects and costumes used in the play should derive from the indicated time and be consistent with it. However, it is possible that those objects and costumes do not define that period exactly. By virtue of careful choices and exclusion of overtly fashionable or stylised objects a more ambiguous sense of period can be generated.

The period and locale of the play have been chosen precisely because they allow a degree of interpretative generality in how the play 'looks'. It is a 'look' that may extend beyond the actual period of the play to cover communities and cultures of the modern, particularly those which are 'outside' the immediate current of ever changing and replaceable commodities.

The aim is to create a question concerning the exactness of the period in particular and the idea of period in general. It has to be stressed, however, that this 'aim' must not be realised at the expense of compromising the integrity of the concrete, historical reality that the action unfolds in. It is our interpretation of this reality which is a question, not the fact of it.

Riccardo Galgani
June 2005

A Nick Hern Book

The Found Man first published in Great Britain as a paperback
original in 2005 by Nick Hern Books Limited, 14 Larden Road,
London W3 7ST in association with the Traverse Theatre, Edinburgh

The Found Man copyright © 2005 Riccardo Galgani

Riccardo Galgani has asserted his right to be identified as
the author of this work

Cover image: Euan Myles

Typeset by Country Setting, Kingsdown, Kent CT14 8ES
Printed and bound in Great Britain by Bookmarque, Croydon,
Surrey

A CIP catalogue record for this book is available from
the British Library

ISBN-13   978 1 85459 895 0
ISBN-10   1 85459 895 3